THE INNER GARDEN

THE INNER GARDEN

MEDITATIONS FOR LIFE FROM 9 TO 90

Maureen Garth

HarperCollins*Publishers*

Published by HarperCollins*Publishers*
HarperCollins*Publishers* (Australia) Pty Limited Group
17–19 Terracotta Drive
Blackburn, Victoria 3130
ACN 008 431 730

First published 1994
Reprinted 1997

Designed by William Hung
Cover illustration by Carol Bertuch
Typeset in Galliard by Bookset Pty Ltd
Printed in Australia by McPherson's Printing Group

The National Library of Australia
Cataloguing-in-Publication data:

Garth, Maureen.
The inner garden: meditations for life from 9 to 90.

ISBN 1 86371 329 8

1. Meditation. 2. Meditations. I. Title.

158.12

Contents

For
Eleanor

Who is my light and who taught me
the meaning of love

Introduction

The Value of Meditation

Meditation can give us the strength, purpose and direction which we need in our lives. It is a wonderful calming tool which can help us face the day, relieve stress, and feel good about ourselves.

Meditation is a very soothing, relaxing way of coping with the stress and anxiety of daily life. It gives us the opportunity to let go of everything around us. By using this form of relaxation, we can bring stillness and quietude into busy lives. When we sit quietly, we enter an altered state of consciousness where we benefit from going into the "silence". Meditation slows the heartbeat and lowers the blood pressure.

Meditation can enhance your daily life and living. It can make you more conscious of your surroundings, more aware of people and their needs, more tolerant of the failings of others, and more forgiving of your own failings. Different avenues open up for you to work on yourself while in the meditative state.

Perhaps your life is always in a state of flux and stress. Meditation can help to change that. When you go deeply into your altered state, ideas and thoughts will surface that may show you how to deal with problems in a different fashion.

If you meditate early in the morning, you will face the day feeling more centered, peaceful and assured. Your aura of tranquility will have a calming effect upon others whom you meet throughout the day. Meditating at night will help you to relax and unwind and rid yourself of the tensions of the day.

You do not have to spend a lot of time meditating. If you allocate ten to fifteen minutes both morning and evening, you will find the benefits far outweigh the time spent. This is a time for reflection and contemplation, a time to go within. It is not beyond the reach of anyone who can take the time and create the opportunity.

Meditation has always been available to everyone, but perhaps many of us thought it was only for those who were "different" or a "little strange". It seemed to belong to those who desired to sit on a mountain top in contemplation of the higher meaning of life and not to the ordinary individual. But it is for all of us, whether we want to sit on a mountain top or in a comfortable chair at home.

Through meditation you can contact your higher self, find your direction in life, bring peace and serenity into your life, into your soul, into your person.

My own belief is that the higher self is an essence or an energy force which has accumulated the experiences of the many lifetimes spent on this earth. The person on this earth at the present time is but an aspect of this higher level of consciousness. Because the higher self has the knowledge of the problems encountered in the past, it has the ability to help one deal with the problems of the present time. Other belief systems have different explanations for this energy force but most agree on the value of meditation. When you meditate, you are able to enter and move through different levels and make contact with this force or energy.

I believe in receiving guidance from my higher self and also from people who exist on a different plane. I refer to them as guides. Sometimes when you meditate you "see" people in your garden who speak with you and give you spiritual guidance. They may also speak about what is happening in your physical life. The spiritual and physical are linked, and one cannot exist without the other.

Meditation enables us to get in touch with the spiritual depths of our being, in a place where there is peace and serenity. If our inner being is serene, imagine how we can project this serenity into our lives and onto other people.

Meditation can give us stability. We are made up of physical, mental, emotional and spiritual components and we should take the time to nourish our body, mind, emotions and the spiritual essence within, our higher self. My belief is that our higher self has unlimited wisdom and love and is there to help us if we allow it to and if we trust in it. During meditation it is possible to communicate with this aspect of oneself, to listen, and receive guidance and advice.

Meditation is not new. People have practised meditation throughout the ages in many different cultures. It is used in churches, Buddhist temples, ashrams, mosques and synagogues, in homes or communing with nature in the open air. Although each of the major belief systems meditates in a different way, all come back to going within, to listening to the inner self, to becoming in tune with the self and nature. Some people like to meditate to a mantra, to a sound, to quiet music, to prayer. And others require nothing but silence.

Our body is both male and female. The left side of the body is female and the right side male. In the brain it is reversed—right side female, left side male. The male, or left, side of the brain is the logical side, the one that dictates order and symmetry in life. The left side of the brain can sometimes be too logical and not allow the intuitive and creative right side much latitude. Meditation brings into use the right, or female, side of the brain and allows it to be creative, to be intuitive, and to create the pictures or images of whom you want to be and how you want life to develop.

Creative people are very right-brained, and their creativity flows because they are so in tune with their feminine side. The logical left side can be very pushy and demand we not be airy fairy and that we think constructively. What is needed, of course, is for both sides to work well together, each allowing the other its own space. We spend most of our waking hours being logical and in control. When we meditate we allow ourselves to experience a beautiful creative energy that we may not have felt before.

Meditation in My Life

I learned how to meditate in my late thirties and I have reaped the benefits of going within, or "going into the silence", ever since. So, although it is preferable to learn early, it is never too late for those of us who were not taught the art of listening quietly to the inner self.

I have been using meditation as a tool for some years. It has influenced not only my own life, but the upbringing of my daughter

Eleanor. A few years after her advent into this world in 1981 I was worried by a series of nightmares which she suffered. So I formulated, over a period of time, a series of meditations that gave both of us pleasure (which shows we are never too old nor too young to acknowledge that small child within).

Initially I "gave" her a Guardian Angel with large golden wings so that she would feel protected and secure. I added a garden where we could do many things—ride with the animals, go inside trees, fly with the fairies, board a cloud and drift above the world. I realized that little ones often have worries of which we are unaware, so I added the Worry Tree. I filled her heart with love for all people and all creatures great and small. I "gave" her the light from a star and helped her to feel her small body pulsating with this beautiful light. Thus began the Star Prelude.

Later, the head mistress of Eleanor's infant school asked if I would teach meditation to the second class children. I must admit to a certain amount of trepidation. I was uncertain how a large group of children would react, but I was agreeably surprised.

The feedback from the children was very positive and I felt rewarded by the way they adapted to the meditations. Anything we can do to help children is worth considering and meditation can be very fruitful. Nothing can substitute for the love which we give our children, but we need to reinforce their sense of security within themselves so they are not entirely dependent upon our love and presence.

Because of my experiences with children, both at home and at school, I wrote my first book *Starbright, meditations for children*. I followed this with *Moonbeam, a book of meditations for children*. These books are collections of meditations for adults to read to children. Children love having images drawn for them and they become involved in their meditations; they become the Star Fairy or talk to the Grandfather Tree, or float on their own personal cloud.

When I wrote *Starbright* and *Moonbeam*, I stressed the importance for children to start meditation as early as possible and I still advocate this as a wonderful experience. If started at an early age, meditation can be a natural adjunct to children's lives, even becoming part of normal daily life.

The comments I received from adults were interesting. They too enjoyed the meditations and benefited a lot from them. Eve, a friend's mother in her eighties in England, said that if she couldn't sleep she would read or think of one of the meditations from my book and then drift off. Rhonda said the intensity of the white light from the star increased the quality of her meditations and she found this light very powerful. Others found they drifted into the meditative state with their children and felt better for it.

A journalist interviewing me said she had never been able to meditate but, before writing about *Moonbeam*, she felt she should try the exercises. She brought the light from the Star down and was amazed to find she could feel the light entering her body. When she brought the angel's wings around her she experienced not only the sensation of the feathers, but even their bony structure. Needless to say, she was very excited and I am sure she will have more delightful experiences as she opens herself up to meditation.

These comments prompted me to write *The Inner Garden* as a book of meditations for all who would like to experience the meditative state.

Meditation, Imagination and Visualization

Meditation means going to a place within where you are in contact with your spiritual essence. People who are serious about meditation choose a certain time of the day and faithfully sit at that time; they do not allow anything to interfere. Meditation helps them to face the day in a calmer, more complete way than before; it will help you too.

After you have been sitting for a period of time, you will find yourself going deeper and deeper within, and you may find you will want to stay in the meditative state for a longer period of time. There is no set time. My suggestion of a short period morning and evening is only that, a suggestion. If you feel an hour will bring you more benefits, then by all means spend that time. You will know what is the right length of time for you.

Meditation can help you in many ways and I think you will be surprised at how relaxed you will feel if you put time aside in the morning to meditate. Meditation will not make your problems go away but it often gives you a different approach to them and a calmness and serenity which might otherwise be lacking. Your focus changes and some of the things that have worried or irritated you take on a different perspective.

If you put time aside at night, you will feel calm and serene and very much in tune with yourself thus ensuring a good night's sleep.

If you learn to meditate daily, you are setting up good habits which will stand you in good stead for the day and the future, which could help you become more focussed and centered.

For many of us, these habits were not formed at an early age but it is never too late to learn. If we take the time to meditate once or twice a day, these habits will carry us forward throughout our lives with an ease that can be taken for granted. Some of the benefits can be a peacefulness within and a sense of serenity that may be difficult to attain otherwise.

Meditation can also be combined with imagination and visualization. Some people may think that imagining, or "daydreaming", is an unrealistic way to spend time. What they do not realize is that imagining is a form of meditation. Imagination is creative. Without imagination, there would be no books written, no paintings painted. People who create art or who are pioneers in industry, people who climb mountains, use their imagination to create thoughts, ideas and images which they then activate. They are often meditating, knowingly or unknowingly, and they bring their images together while in the meditative state.

Visualization is different to imagination. Visualization means putting thoughts and images into a more concrete form where we actively work on the images. By meditating in this way we create a scene or an image within ourselves with which we can work to benefit our everyday life.

We close our eyes and see our thoughts transferred into scenes which project our closest desires. Perhaps we are about to sit for an exam. In our daydream, or quiet time, we see projected the result of what we would like to attain. We see ourselves sitting with the test paper in front of us, writing the answers, pausing every so often to collect our thoughts, and then speaking or writing the correct answers. Our mind progresses further. We see the results being announced, and we feel the joy of knowing we have succeeded.

What we are doing is setting up a scenario which, if we have a strong enough belief in what we are visualizing, can be played back into real life. Our daydreaming can be constructive and not time wasting. Our creativity can flow when we daydream. Our thoughts can wander from our present limited pattern to a more relaxed and developed way of looking at what we want in life.

Meditation is a beautiful way of harnessing these creative impulses and energies. It gives us peace and quiet as we settle, and yet we can create the images which we would most like reflected into our "normal" life.

I believe we can use meditation to visualize what we need to have in our lives, whether it be strength, love of life or people, a happier environment, a better place of work, better study skills, or better health. In meditation we go to an inner part of ourselves where, by sitting quietly the breathing slows, the heart quietens, and we learn the answers to our troubles.

Meditation means going within, listening to the inner or higher self, while visualization means using visual pictures in the meditative state to create what you need in your life.

Although meditation and visualization can be used together quite happily, you can also practice them separately. You can use your visualization as you walk around, while doing housework, while travelling on public transport.

Children have a way of thinking and seeing that adults have forgotten. They have no doubt Santa Claus will bring presents. They have no doubt the Easter Bunny will bring eggs. They have no doubt the Tooth Fairy will take their tooth and leave money. So, Santa Claus brings presents, the Easter Bunny the eggs, and the Tooth Fairy the money.

It seems very easy, doesn't it? And I hear you saying, "but that belongs to childhood and the adults make the presents, the eggs, the money, appear". You are quite right, the adults do. But the child's visualization has worked.

Children do not doubt that they deserve these things. We can learn from them. With the advent of growing up, some of us have forgotten how to attain what is necessary to make our lives work for us. It might sound simple to say that if you believe in something strongly enough, you will attain it, but it can work.

Sometimes we do not get what we think we want, either because we have not visualized it strongly enough or because, at some deeper inner level, we know it isn't the right thing for us.

Prior to writing my first book, *Starbright*, I "saw" myself speaking on television about the meditations and how the children responded to them. I was astounded and flattened when it didn't happen. I approached television stations to be told they were inundated with authors and couldn't put me on at that time. I never doubted I would be on television, speaking about my book. I felt quite bewildered when this did not occur when *I* wanted it to. My visualization had been strong and sure and, again, I "knew" it would happen.

So, what went wrong? My timing was off. I expected it to happen immediately the book was published but the television interview occurred some time down the track. And it came about through an article on *Starbright* which appeared in a popular magazine. The TV station saw the article, contact was made, and my visualization became real. Another TV station wanted to do a feature on meditation and my books were mentioned to them by a person unknown to me, again my visualization came true.

I would also like to qualify what else I did to encourage my visualization. I didn't sit back and just think things would come through for me (although they might have). I knew barely anything about the publishing process or how to market myself but I quickly learned how to put myself and my skills forward. I contacted magazines, newspapers, television stations. I offered myself for book signings. Initially I found it difficult to push myself forward but I persisted. And I kept visualizing being in magazines, newspapers, television, doing book signings. And I have had all of these things occur, not just once, but many times. If you have a strong belief system in what you are doing and you apply yourself, and you apply it to your visualization, then why would it not happen? As long as your motives are pure, as long as you do not try to influence another's behavior to your own advantage and their disadvantage, there is no reason why it will not work.

Meditation has helped me in many ways. I have had periods of ill health where, by meditating and using constructive visualization, I have been able to improve my health and change the course of events. I meditated deeply to rid myself of an illness but I also had a strong belief that I could do this. At the same time, I sought medical advice, modified my diet, changed my thinking and the course of the illness changed.

Meditation has brought a lot of joy and peace into my life. Just being able to sit quietly and to feel contact with what I call the "universal energy or being" has enhanced my life.

I have used the meditative state to bring into my life what I feel is required. Sometimes I require very little, but there are times when I ask that my larger needs be met, and invariably they are. This does not mean I have sat back and waited for things to occur. I have actively worked towards attainment of a goal. At the same time I have worked on the meditative level to visualize the goal, to see it coming to pass, and to bring it through into my life.

Life today is very competitive. There is a far greater need to achieve. Going to school, university, work, or even just traveling about, driving a car or on public transport, everything is more stressful now than ever before. We are always in a hurry, there is no time to spare. Running a home and working, running an office and rearing children, being a father, mother, child, or friend, requires commitment and balance. Relationships are constantly changing, again causing pressure on the nervous system.

Getting older, and perhaps not being able to face old age or the fact that we are aging, can cause worry. Sometimes one can see and feel the physical changes but the changes on the inside, on the emotional level, are difficult to explain or focus on. What we feel and what we can express may be two different things. Sometimes it may be very difficult to articulate needs.

In all these stresses of daily life meditation can be beneficial.

Using the Meditations in this Book

I have written what I call the Star Prelude to preface the entry into the garden where all my meditations take place. I ask that you see a Star above your head and bring its light down through your body until you are filled with this light as you sit. There is a Worry Tree which is important because it helps you to go into your meditation with a clear mind. Sometimes you need to take a while before you can really use the tree to its fullest advantage, but it works and it works well.

It is also good to open your heart and fill it with love because we all need to learn to love freely and openly without requiring love in return. In other words, unconditional love. With children I always invite them to feel the wings of an angel wrapped around them. You too could do this, or perhaps imagine there is a wise person or protector with you. No matter how old we are, we need that security. When you come back from the garden, wrap yourself in a golden cloak and send your energy back into the universe to be used for the highest and best.

All of my meditations take place in a lovely garden. This garden is not an external garden, but one that lives inside each of us. It is somewhere you can go which is specifically yours. When you close the gate behind you, you have entered the garden and its peaceful state. There, nothing can harm you; everyone lives together peacefully, including the animals, and nothing ever dies because there is no death.

When you close the garden gate behind you, you can choose

any of the meditations in this book or draw upon images in your own mind. That is how it has always worked for me. You see one thing and it leads to another; or you could take the theme from one of my meditations and develop it in your own style.

Meditation is very simple. You can begin by sitting quietly either on your own or with a group of people. It is best to sit in an upright chair—if you make the chair too comfortable, you may fall asleep. Try to wear loose clothing for comfort but, if that is not possible, loosen anything which is tight around the waist or neck so that you do not feel these restrictions. It is wise not to cross your arms and legs as this can lead to discomfort.

You might like to have soothing music in the background or perhaps you might prefer silence. Sometimes I like to fix a scene in my head, such as my beautiful garden; at other times my mind is like a blank screen ready to receive whatever images happen to cross it.

The brain works at different levels of consciousness. These levels are called Beta, Alpha, Theta and Delta. Beta is the normal conscious level, the level at which we work in our daily lives. When we go into a meditative state we are going into Alpha, the state which enables us to create scenes and images on the screen of our mind. We can attain Theta as we go more deeply into the meditative state. Delta is our sleep level. Most of us work very well within Alpha and come back feeling refreshed and renewed.

It is up to the individual to decide how long to spend in meditation. If you can only spare five or ten minutes that can be ample. However, to feel the full benefit, twenty minutes is better because meditation can promote calmness, relax tension, and give relief from anxiety as you become detached from your problems. Your problems will not necessarily go away, but meditation can be beneficial to the way you handle those problems. Sometimes the solution comes when you take the time to sit quietly.

The meditations in this book are not just pleasant imagery; they are positive tools to be used in:

1 releasing fears
2 attaining a positive attitude
3 problem solving.

Perhaps some of our attitudes have become negative through lack of direction or difficulty in expressing our innermost feelings and thoughts. We may think things are more difficult than they are, but a new perspective on our problems will make them easier to solve.

All the meditations are visually rich and all take place within your personal garden, a garden where nothing can harm you, where there is peace and tranquility. You feel the warmth of the sun caressing you; you hear and see the flowers and the grass growing. You open yourself to each experience, so different each time you enter the meditative state. Your garden exists within you and is always accessible.

Many of the meditations are to relax you and to encourage you to "see" more for yourself. They may bring forth from "the child within" the creativity that has been buried for so long, or the longed for or needed peace.

Some meditations, for example on travel, encourage you to expand your mind, to take in other cultures and experiences. But why stop where I have begun? You could go on a time excursion by expanding the Father Time (p. 109) meditation. You could move backwards or forwards, into dimensions not previously imagined.

Or you could relax, take the meditations as they are written, then you do not have to do any work at all. Simply let the meditations waft over you.

Each meditation is different and should not restrict you in any way. Allow yourself to flow with them, to enter into them, to enjoy them. Bring back each experience as a new experience for you, and allow the peace and tranquility to flow through your day, every day.

In The Mountain (p. 104), you are given choices on how to reach the top of the mountain, and afterwards how to increase your size so that the mountain appears small. Why do we have to accept that we are small in comparison to the mountain? Mountains, or problems, are something to overcome. A difference in perspective can help us to identify the problem and resolve it.

Approaching exams, driving tests, interviews, can be very stressful and there is a lot of fear associated with them. Am I good enough? Will I remember all I have learned? In School (p. 90) and Exams (p. 95), you will find a positive formula which could be helpful in approaching such situations.

The Colors of Healing meditation (p. 135) shows how you could concentrate on those areas of the body which need healing. Meditating, using colors and visualization, is a great aid in the healing process.

The Boulevard of Broken Dreams (p. 130) takes us into our past to heal the past. It helps to release what we are still holding close to ourselves, the guilt, the pain. Perhaps there are issues that we are clinging to which need to be looked at, and then put to rest.

Meditating Alone

Decide whether you prefer to meditate in the early morning or late evening, or both, when you feel you will be free of interruptions. If you find midday the best time, make yourself comfortable, relax, but take the phone off the hook and don't have anything going on in the kitchen which will sound alarms. You don't have to meditate for long periods of time but, if you are the type of person who goes very deeply and would rather stay in the meditative state but haven't the time, fix a return time firmly in your mind. You will find that you will.

Even though you are alone, begin with the Star Prelude, taking the light from the Star down through the body. Work on your heart, leaving your worries on the Worry Tree, joining the Wise Person and then going into one of the meditations. Read the meditation through to fix it in your mind; sit and relax and let your mind ponder the selected meditation, perhaps changing it to suit your personality or how you are feeling at the time. When you come back, please remember to wrap your golden cloak around you and send back the energy you have been using into the universe for the highest and best.

Group Meditation

I have taught meditation for some years. I invite groups to sit in a circle on straight-backed chairs, relaxing body and mind, loosening any tight clothing and taking off shoes if necessary. Although it is not mandatory, it is a good idea to remove jangly jewellery and avoid strong perfume. These can interfere with the other sitters whose senses are heightened or who may be allergy prone.

I introduce the Star Prelude (see p. 25), and then I take the group to a place in the meditation where I leave them for a period of approximately forty-five to sixty minutes, depending upon how settled they are and how I feel. The length of time is up to the leader—if you feel half an hour is sufficient, then that is the right length of time for you and them. When the group is new, it is perhaps best to start with a shorter time and gradually lengthen it.

When I bring the group out, I do so from the place in the meditation where I left them. I take them back along the path to the gate, close it behind them firmly, and tell them to open their eyes when they are ready.

Some people take longer than others to come back. If you feel some are staying in the meditative state for too long, call them by name and tell them to return. Sometimes when we go very deeply, we want to stay there. However, life beckons and goes on, and so we must come back.

I wrap each person in a lovely golden cloak to close them off from the meditation level. I bring this cloak down over the top of the head, wrapping it around the body until it comes below the feet. I also send the energy back into the universe to be used for the highest and the best.

If you decide to meditate as a group, it is important that you feel comfortable with each other. Sitting with someone who makes you uncomfortable, can interfere with your meditation and vice versa. However, I am sure that if you decide to set up a group, you will have only those with whom you are compatible.

When sitting in a group, you will find that the group energy can make it easier to meditate and to see things in your relaxed state. Choose a day and time suitable to all and keep to that time schedule. Do not allow other things to take you away from your weekly meditation group. The consistent attendance will bring many benefits to all of you.

There must be one person to lead the meditation. Normally it is best for the same person to lead the group each week, but you could perhaps take turns. Such rotation gives leaders a chance to hone visualization or imaginative skills and to make each meditation entirely their own.

The person who leads the meditation will not be able to meditate as deeply as perhaps they would like. They have to be aware at all times and able to bring the others back at the appropriate time. If the leader drifts off too far, who will bring the group back?

You might think, when you read, that the meditations are not very long. Please remember that when you are speaking to a group, you will do so in a very slow, relaxed voice, pausing to let the scene sink in. Then the group, sitting with eyes closed and focussing inward, can easily visualize and feel the scene. The way the leader uses their voice is very important. It is best to drop the voice by a few tones and speak more and more slowly, with a soothing quality. There is a hypnotic quality about a low and relaxed voice that can help people into the meditative state.

Making the Meditations Your Own

What I have written, be it the Star Prelude or any of the meditations, has been written only as a guide. You may make any of them your own. Perhaps by doing so you will bring to mind details which I have not included.

The Star Prelude

I WANT you to see above your head a beautiful, beautiful Star which is filled with white light, lovely white light which shimmers and glows. I want you to see this light streaming down towards you until it reaches the very top of your head. And now I want you to bring this pure light down through your head and take it right down your body until it is filled with this glorious white light.

I want you to feel the light going down your

arms, right down, until you feel it reaching your hands and going into each and every finger.

Feel that light going down the trunk of your body, down until it reaches your legs and when you feel it there, take it right down until it comes to your feet and then feel the light going through each toe.

Now that you have brought this glorious light down, you are a beacon of light and have become as a living flame.

Look into your heart and fill your heart with love for all people and for all creatures, great and small. Can you see your heart getting bigger and bigger? It's expanding because you have so much love in your heart for all people, and the animals, and of course for yourself.

Before you enter your garden, I want you to look at the large tree outside. This tree is called the "Worry Tree". I want you to pin on this tree anything which might worry you—perhaps you have problems with work, or maybe you are having difficulties in your personal life. This tree will take any worries at all, no matter how small or how large. This tree accepts anything that you would care to pin or place there.

In front of you there is a Wise Person who has been waiting patiently for you to come, who will always care for and protect you. Can you feel the love emanating from this special person towards you? Or perhaps you have a Guardian Angel who will wrap golden wings of protection around you before taking you into your garden. The Angel's wings are very large and very soft, just like down. Everyone has their own Guardian Angel or Wise Person who takes care of you and protects you always, so you are never alone. It's important to remember this and to know that you have someone who looks after you with love and care.

Take the hand that is extended, open the gate before you and enter your garden, closing the gate firmly behind you. As you do, the colors spring to life, colors like nothing you have seen before. The beauty of the flowers, the colors, the textures and the perfume—breathe them in. The grass is a vivid green and the sky a beautiful blue with white fluffy clouds. It is very peaceful in your garden; it is full of love and harmony.

Freeing the Mind

Some meditations are to allow the mind to flow, to roam, to feel free, to experience the images which form in the mind.

The Rose brings fairies into our consciousness, and can take you into the inner world of the rose or any flower you choose.

The Cave Dwellers takes you high above your normal space and allows that perhaps there might be other species of which you are unaware.

The Castle takes you into a magical place where there is a special room, just for you.

Flying allows you to become a bird and to fly high into the heavens and to feel the freedom of flight.

The Rose

YOUR GARDEN feels fresh and clear as you enter, and the gentle breeze sends its light fingers through your hair. As you go down your pathway, you see before you the most beautiful rose you have ever seen. It is deep pink and the petals show no signs of bruising. It is as if the rose bush burst forth from the ground in a pure unblemished state.

There are dew drops glistening on the petals,

reflecting the light from the warmth of the sun, and changing the color slightly.

The rose looks very inviting as it moves its outer petals in the light breeze. Why don't you become small enough to enter the rose? Feel yourself shrinking until you are very, very tiny, and the rose in front of you seems very, very large.

Feel the satin softness of the petals as you pull them aside so that you can walk into the rose. Walk around the outside petals first. Then go around and around, until you come closer to the rose's centre. Take your time. You will come across many insects and ants who live in the rose. They appear to be very busy, rushing backwards and forwards, and talking to each other. Can you hear what they are saying?

The perfume is becoming stronger as you near the centre of the rose. At first it makes you feel a little giddy until you become used to it. Now you are at the heart of the rose. The petals are opening out further so that you can sit inside the rose, feeling the warmth of the sun on your body and the lightness of the air surrounding you.

There is dew on the petals; perhaps a drop will fall on you. Shake yourself and allow the water to splash back onto the velvet petals.

Why don't you lie down and enjoy the perfume of the rose as it gently surrounds you. There are bees going from rose to rose and perhaps one will land near you. Now that you are so small, perhaps you could climb on to the back of the bee and fly with him as he takes the pollen from each flower . . .

Or you may prefer to linger in the rose. The petals are opening back further and now you can watch the rose fairies flying from rose to rose. Each rose has its own special fairy. The white roses have fairies who are dressed all in white and gold, while the red fairies' dresses match the red of the rose. They wear rubies in their hair. The yellow fairies have gold dresses and their delicate wings are tipped with gold. The pink fairies have small pink roses entwined through their hair. Their dresses are shot with silver and gold, changing into lighter and darker shades of pink as they move.

These fairies work with the roses to make sure their perfume is just right. If the perfume isn't strong enough, they loosen the top of the stem underneath the rose's head so that the perfume flows better. If the smell is too strong, they tighten it.

Why don't you go and help them with their work? It would be lovely to fly from rose to rose helping to adjust the fragrances . . .

The Cave Dwellers

BREATHE **IN** the smell of the mountain air that surrounds your garden. It is fresh and delightful and touches you gently on the face and body.

The mountains are all around you, but one seems to beckon to you more than the others. It is not as difficult as it might at first seem to climb a mountain. You have strong boots on your feet and you certainly will not feel the cold with the warm clothing you are wearing; and your back pack is filled with food and drink.

As you walk up the mountain, you will notice on the pathway the rock formations and the wild flowers growing between the rock crevices. Up and up you go, feeling very sure footed. As you go higher and higher, the air is becoming fresher, but you do not feel the cold.

When you look down, you will be surprised to see how far you have come. If you look up, you will see that you have not very far to go before you reach the top of the mountain.

Can you see what is at the very top? It's a white mountain goat. She is very graceful as she leaps from rock to rock without faltering. She is a sure footed animal and loves to live high in the mountains. Keep your eye on the goat and try to reach where she is. Perhaps you can be as nimble and sure footed as she is.

Have you seen the cave which is set back from the pathway? It is not clear to everyone but your sharp eyes don't miss much. Why don't you enter this cave to rest a little?

Feel the warmth as you enter. The smell of dry earth mixes with the freshness of the air. It is not dark. Your eyes can see that there are more caves opening out of this one. I hear movement—can you? Perhaps you could go further into the cave to see who is there.

Why, there are people who live in these caves

and they are called Cave Dwellers. Did you know that Cave Dwellers are very shy and receive few visitors because they live high in the mountains? Most people who climb the pathway rarely seem to notice the cave.

The Cave Dwellers take care of the mountains and the small animals that live there. Would you like to stay with them? They would love to have your company.

When you are ready, they would like to take you to the crest of the mountain. I am sure you will love the feeling of being at the very top of the world with the limitless sky above and space surrounding you . . .

The Castle

YOU CAN hear the light breeze rustling through the leaves of the many trees that are in your garden. The flowers are pushing their heads forward to catch the sun's golden rays.

There are many things in your garden, many things that you have not yet explored. Have you ever wondered what it is like to live in a castle? It could be exciting to live there and perhaps you could, even if it is only for a little while.

Can you see the castle sitting on the mountain top? It has many turrets that reach into the sky, and it is surrounded by a moat. To get there you could take the ski lift or perhaps you could catch the small train which takes you up the mountainside. You may even decide to climb the mountain. I am sure this will not be difficult, because you can do whatever you set your mind to.

And now you are there in front of the most magnificent castle you have ever seen. The drawbridge is down for you to cross. The moat is filled with water where golden fish swim and white and black swans glide by.

In front of you is an enormous wooden door. Ask the door to open and it will swing back on its hinges, allowing you to enter.

The rooms are huge with high ceilings and filled with many different things. The chairs and tables are ornate and the paintings on the walls are of many people you know. The multi-colored glass in the windows seems to change as the sun's rays pass through it.

Look, there is a winding staircase to take you to the bedrooms on the next floor. On this level is one special room for you only. It is not for anyone else, just for you. This room is filled with all the things you like, and all the things you think you would like. No one can enter this room unless you give them permission. In this room you can be on your own if you want, or invite people to share with you.

Perhaps you might like now to go into the

turrets of the castle. This staircase is even narrower and more winding but when you reach the top, you can see for miles around. I think I will leave you there . . .

Flying

THE BRANCHES of the large trees in your garden are bending and moving as they feel the breeze gently ruffling their leaves. They are shaking themselves ever so slightly. The many birds that have made their homes there, take off.

Watch the birds flying and you will see how they dip and soar through the air. They appear to be weightless and can do anything they want. With a slight motion of their wings, they go up or down. If they decide to land, they fix in their mind the point of landing and adjust their speed to where they want to go.

Have you thought about being a bird? It must be lovely to feel the freedom of flight, the air rushing by as you go higher and higher, always searching, always looking further ahead.

Why don't you become an eagle? They have such firm strong bodies and their wings have a large span from tip to tip.

Feel yourself flying as the eagle flies, the cool, clean air surrounding you. You are now so high you are breaking through the clouds which leave a light residue of mist on your feathers as you pass through them. The world on the other side of the clouds is clear and shining and beautiful.

Circle above the clouds for a while in a lazy way. Take your time as you dip and glide. Pull yourself up and then propel yourself downward through the clouds, until you can see the earth.

Fly slowly above the earth as you search for the eagle's home. Can you see it? It is perched high on top of a mountain. Bring yourself down, fanning your wings out in all their glory, feeling the air rustling the feathers on your body and wings, and smoothing the feathers on the crest of your head.

Lower yourself slowly into the nest with its very hungry babies. Their mouths are open as they wait for food. Their noises indicate their hunger.

The nestlings are not very strong yet because they are small, but soon they will be as wise and as large as you. When they are, you can take them flying, soaring and lifting through the air, away from the nest.

But for now they are hungry. Perhaps you should go searching for food to bring to these little ones . . .

Travel and Other Boundaries

The meditations on travel are not just for armchair travellers who have been physically unable to go to the countries concerned (although this is an agreeable way to travel). These meditations allow the mind to travel, to go through time and space, to move and not stand still. They allow the mind to see, to hear, to feel, to smell, to push aside boundaries that are limiting. Allow yourself to feel free, to wander, and to take advantage of the limitless feeling that these meditations bring.

The Sun and its Light takes you out of this world and into the solar system.

The World takes you to Africa and its amazing countryside and animals.

In **Egypt** you will find your clothes are Egyptian and your camel will take you across the hot sands to the pyramids.

America takes you to modern America and then back in time to when the Indians and buffalo ruled.

Italy allows you to experience some of the beautiful cities that abound there.

Ayers Rock shows an amazing rock that is a sacred site which has many drawings depicting the culture of the Australian Aboriginal people.

The Sun and its Light

THE SUN is sending its light into your garden.
You can feel the warmth of its rays caressing your
body as the light breeze moves through your hair.
The light is dappling through the trees and settling
around the flowers, enhancing their beauty.
The white gardenia tree is sending its beautiful
perfume to mingle with that of the magnolia tree.
The flowers in their many colors of pink, purple,
yellow and red, are standing proud and tall while

the sun's rays pour around them, encouraging them to grow.

Very tiny puffs of clouds are scudding across the beautiful azure blue sky. The sun hangs in the sky like a giant golden ball, spreading its light out to all who care to feel it.

Look around you. Do you notice the many deer coming through the trees and the rabbits emerging from their burrows. They love to feel the sun on their fur.

Feel the warmth of the sun and luxuriate in its glow. These gentle rays are permeating your body, making you feel stronger and more energetic than you have been for some time.

The sun is directing one of its rays to where

you stand and it is coming to rest at your feet. Why don't you stand within this ray of light and allow yourself to be lifted up? The light will take you higher and higher, and you will feel the gentle warmth which surrounds your body, holding and transporting you to the body of the sun.

This ray of light is allowing you to step off onto the sun itself. The intensity of the sun's warmth has been sent out for the light of the world, leaving a gentleness that allows you to walk on the surface of the sun.

Being on the sun is unlike anything you have experienced before. It is almost as though the strength of the sun is controlled through a network of beams crossing each other, permitting the light to shine forth where it is most needed.

There are people living on the sun who control the beams of light that enrich the lives of so many. Perhaps you could go to these people of light and warmth. They show you how you were transported to the sun, the centre of the solar system. And perhaps, you could go further afield . . .

The World

THERE **IS** a hushed air of expectancy in your garden as you enter. The animals are sitting close to the trunks of the many trees and the flowers are waving their heads, creating a rainbow of color.

The air is still and calm and makes you feel you would like to travel and see the world. It is a wonderful experience, one which you will thoroughly enjoy.

Most people travel—by train, by boat, by aeroplane—or by walking the long distances between countries, but for now you can travel in a different way to anyone else.

Stand on a grassy spot in your garden and feel your feet lift off the ground. You don't need special wings nor a plane, unless you would like to have either. Your body will float through the air, rising higher and higher above the earth. Doesn't it look strange when you look down? It doesn't look very big at all.

As you hover above the earth, you will notice a bright light coming from one particular place. That is the one you will visit. Feel the soft air holding you and touch the clouds as you pass them on your way down to the spot you have chosen.

And I do believe you have chosen a game park. As you come closer to earth, you will notice the trees and the grass are quite different to those at your home. Some parts are dry and other parts are very green. There are many animals milling about on these wide open spaces. There are rhinoceros and elephants enjoying a bath in the river, and deer with their little ones are drinking the water.

Lying on a large rock overlooking the river and the plains is a family of lions. Why don't you fly down and join them on the rock? Their fur coats are rough but beautifully warm and they love being stroked.

The lions have three small cubs who are very playful. They are falling over each other trying to get near you to be patted. The sun's warmth has entered the rock and it feels wonderful to sit there with these lions and their cubs. You might want to stay for a time.

From where you are sitting, you can see the waterhole where the animals gather each evening. There are rhinoceros, giraffes, and elephants. Monkeys are swinging from branch to branch, laughing in their shrill voices. The zebra are coming and the buffalo kick up a cloud of dust in the distance as they come towards the other animals.

Perhaps you may decide to join the animals in the water, or maybe you might like to stay with the big cats on the warm rock and watch the animals below. It is up to you . . .

Egypt

THE AIR is warm around you, and the trees are sending shade to the sheltering animals. There is a stillness that makes you feel as though you could transport yourself to another time, another land.

Feel yourself leaving your garden, flying higher and higher, and then drifting through the limitless blue sky, touching the occasional wisp of white cloud, until you see a spot where you want to land.

You are surrounded by sand, endless golden sand that shimmers in the sun's rays. You have taken yourself into the desert of Egypt. You will notice that your clothing has changed and you are wearing Egyptian garments. Long robes protect your body against the sun's rays and the head-dress falls from the top of your head to your shoulders.

There is a camel coming towards you. Over his hump hangs a blanket patterned in red and orange. There are reins dangling from his mouth and long stirrups swing below the hump. Put your foot into the stirrup and pull yourself onto his back so that you can take the reins in your hands and place your foot in the other stirrup.

It is a funny feeling, lurching up and down on the camel's back, quite different to being on a horse.

The camel's long legs are speeding across the sand, taking you to an oasis where there are clusters of palm trees and a cool pond for you to bathe. Try the dates if you are hungry or join the other travellers who are resting there before going on their journey.

Everyone is now preparing to leave the oasis. The camels are coming forward for the travellers to mount. I think you might join these people because they plan on going further across the sands to see what the rest of Egypt is like.

The sun is beaming down but your clothes are keeping the heat from you and the air cools you as your camel picks up speed to stay with the others.

In the distance you can see a strange structure with four corners rising to a peak in the middle. It is one of the many pyramids which the ancient Egyptians built as a memorial to their kings. Many large stones were used to build these pyramids.

If you look closely, you will see a small entrance high up which will take you inside. Climb up until you are able to enter. Inside it is cool, with a slight musty smell, and there is a narrow staircase which will take you up into the centre of the pyramid. Why don't you go up this staircase? When you get there, you will find a tomb where the king was laid to rest. People left many jewels and presents for the king and you could look at them. There are head-dresses, ornate necklaces, rings with large colored stones, and bracelets; many, many things.

When you are tired of looking at the king's resting place and jewels, come down the stairs and out onto the side of the pyramid. You can see a huge statue not far from this pyramid. It is a strange statue. It looks like a lion but it has the head of a human. Why, I believe it's the Sphinx. Go closer and you will see how large it is in comparison to yourself. I wonder how it was built? It must have taken many people and many stones . . .

America

THE SUN hangs like a giant golden globe in the sky, and the trees move gently with the light breeze. The perfume of the flowers drifts around you as the large white cloud comes from above to land at your feet. Why don't you step onto this cloud and see where it takes you?

Your cloud is taking you far, far away, until it hovers over a collection of buildings, and then gently comes in to land. The first thing you notice is the Statue of Liberty standing proudly erect in the water just outside the city of New York. She has been there for many years and is admired by many people as a symbol of freedom.

You could land on her head if you like. Land like a bird lightly touching down. Look around and you will see the skyscrapers standing erect, reaching for the sky, each of them trying to outstrip their neighbors in their height. You could fly from this statue to the Empire State Building and land on the top floor. From here you will have yet another view of New York and the people who live there. From where you are, they look very small, don't they?

Why don't you leave New York and fly across

America, landing in all the cities and towns that appeal to you.

You could even take yourself back in time and look at the land as it used to be a long time ago, when the first people roamed the country.

Can you see a group of people living together? There is smoke rising from their fires. Why don't you land near the largest tent, or tepee. There is no need to rattle the beads that hang outside the opening. They have been expecting you.

The chief is coming out. His name is Running Deer. He is wearing his headdress today, the one which is full of feathers. He is holding out his hands in welcome and is offering you a Peace Pipe. You don't have to smoke it of course, but take the pipe

from his hand and thank him for sharing it
with you.

Running Deer is calling for his men to gather
up the horses because he wants to take you riding.
You can choose any horse you like—the strong
black one that is throwing his head back as he rears
up into the air, or perhaps the white one anxiously
pawing at the ground, eager to get started. Or
maybe you would like a piebald pony, one of many
colors?

Swing yourself onto the horse's back and away
you go, thundering across the plains until you reach
a high cliff. Running Deer is holding his hand up
for you to halt. Be quiet for the moment as he
points out the large herd of buffalo running below.
These magnificent beasts have their heads down as

they surge ahead, raising a cloud of dust that lingers behind them.

Running Deer wants to show you how to send smoke signals to communicate with another camp. He is sending a message asking that Strong Eagle, who belongs to a different group of people, bring his men to meet you. Why don't you wait for them to arrive?

Italy

FEEL THE freshness of the air caressing your cheeks, ruffling your hair, surrounding your body. It makes you want to fly, to take off, to soar through the air. See yourself flying around the world. You do not need an aeroplane for you can fly without mechanical means. You do not need wings either, but if you would rather, then feel them sprouting from your back until you have two beautifully formed feathered wings to take you on your travels.

Because you are flying on your own, you do not need to make arrangements as to where you would like to go. Look at the world as you glide past, and choose a spot on the globe that appeals to you for a visit.

Perhaps it might be Japan—or England—or could it be the continent of Europe? Or perhaps it could be Egypt or America again. The world is there at your feet and it is your choice. You will have many times when you can fly around the world, selecting your next port of call, but for the moment, you might like to land in Italy.

See yourself landing in St Peter's Square at the

Vatican City in Rome. The square is full of people waiting to enter St Peter's to look at this vast and wonderful ancient church, with its many beautiful paintings and statues. If you stay in the square outside, the Pope may come and give his blessings to the people who have gathered there.

You could then go to the Coliseum where people fought the lions in days long past for what they believed in. It is empty now except for people like yourself with inquiring minds.

Why don't you leave Rome and go to Florence where Michelangelo carved the beautiful statue of David? There are many magnificent statues in Florence which exist side by side with the colorful markets where the Italians sell everything from ice cream to handbags and furnishings.

From Florence you could fly to Venice, lowering yourself into a gondola so that you can drift along the waterways learning more of this beautiful city. Perhaps you may care to watch the glass blowers as they create their delicate wares, blowing and spinning the glass to make intricate patterns which are a feature of the beautifully colored Venetian glass.

You may decide to stay in Venice for a while, or go elsewhere in your travels, perhaps back to Florence or to a new city, perhaps even to Milan to enter their beautiful opera house and to listen to music such as you have never heard before . . .

Ayers Rock

THERE IS a feeling of something different in your garden. The sun hangs overhead like a rich golden globe, filled with a warm light which is bathing you in its gentle glow. The sky is a rich sapphire blue hung with the merest wisps of cloud.

There are many animals around, but this time they are all native Australian animals. There are koalas, emus, kangaroos and platypus. There are some baby koalas clinging to the backs of their mothers. And look at the kangaroo—the small joey is popping his head in and out of her pouch. He has now decided to stay looking out and his paws are dangling over the side.

The emus are strange looking creatures, aren't they? Their necks are long and their legs are like sticks, but their bodies are big with large feathers. You may want to get onto the back of an emu and be taken for a ride to a place which is very special to the Aboriginal people of Australia.

The other animals are following as the emu's long legs take you quickly toward Ayers Rock, the biggest red rock in the world. It is so long and wide that it would take you hours to walk around its base. If you decide to climb the rock, be prepared to hold onto the rope very tightly as you go up. It is very steep and quite a long way to go.

Ayers Rock changes color at sunrise and sunset. You can see it changing from red to brown as the sun's rays fall on it, and then into a delicate purple which becomes stronger as the light alters. Look now and you will see the rock is a brilliant golden yellow standing proudly against the skyline; then shortly it will turn a rich burnished orange. As the light fades or moves, Ayers Rock returns to its natural rich red beauty in a sparse landscape.

As you slide off your emu's back, you will see a group of dark skinned people. They are the Aboriginal people who live at Ayers Rock. They wear a small cloth around their hips and their chests and faces are painted in patterns of white. The men lean on their spears as they wait for you to approach.

They have been waiting for you, waiting to dress you too in a small red cloth, and to paint you in their ceremonial style.

Ayers Rock, or Uluru in their language, is a sacred place to the Aboriginal people and it is loved by them. There are caves in this rock that no one can enter unless they have been initiated in the ways of the Aboriginal people who live there. Because they have painted you and given you a loin cloth, they consider you their friend and one of them.

They are taking you into one of the caves that is hidden from view by a few bushes. When you go inside and your eyes adjust to the light, they will show you the wall paintings which depict their culture. Some paintings have been there for thousands of years. Perhaps they have some paints made up and would show you how to draw and paint as they do. Would you like to try?

When you feel you would like to come outside, your Aboriginal friends will take you to a special part of Ayers Rock that is called "The Brain". The tribal elder will show you how this rock is pitted by time and nature and how these marks have formed a pattern which looks very much like the human brain.

Each Aboriginal man has a boomerang and a didgeridoo. The tribal elder has two of each and he is offering to show you how to throw the boomerang so that it will return to you, and also how to play the didgeridoo.

Some men may join you in playing the didgeridoo while the native animals sit and watch. Perhaps the children will perform a ceremonial dance. You may like to join them in their dancing. What do you think?

Creativity

Perhaps you have never played the piano or painted. Maybe you have always wanted to run your fingers across the keys or to have paint splattered across your clothes but felt you didn't have the ability. While you meditate, you can experience these things. Perhaps your meditations might encourage you to learn. . .

You need not restrict yourself to the content of the following meditations of course. You could adapt them to anything that is creative. We all have unused abilities and perhaps these meditations will encourage you to use some of yours.

The Easel and **The Piano** show how you can feel the picture you wish to depict forming on the canvas, and how your hands bring the music from the ivory keys.

Perfection shows how to fulfil your dream: to see yourself accepting awards, being applauded for what you have accomplished.

The Easel

I WANT you to walk along the garden path, feeling the sun on your back. The gentle breeze is ruffling your hair as you climb to the top of a hill. When you stand on the top of this hill you can see far, far away, as far as the eye can see.

Below you is a valley with a shining river. A few horses graze beside the river, taking shade and shelter from the large trees which are gently spreading their branches along the river bank. Cows and sheep are nearby, standing deep in the rich green grass.

In the distance are huge mountains with snow-covered peaks. A few clouds are resting on the top of the mountains. Some look like berets whilst the others look like skirts clinging to the rocky slopes. You feel you want to paint this scene.

If you look just a little behind you, you will find an artist's easel has already been set up with a canvas prepared for painting. You will find every color you need, and every brush you could possibly want. There are lots of rags to wipe your hands on. Artists get paint on their hands and even sometimes on their faces. You needn't worry about getting your clothing dirty though, because you have a

painter's smock to wear and a red beret for
your head.

You can now sit on the seat by your easel and
you can paint onto the canvas the majestic scene in
front of you. You can draw and paint as much as
you like. Indeed you can paint to your heart's
delight, putting big splashy colors in some places
and tiny ones in others.

And then, if you feel a little tired, you can lie
down to enjoy the sun and the scenery . . .

The Piano

THE TREES are waving their arms in welcome as you enter your garden and they are showing you the way to a clearing. Many animals have come to this clearing and are sitting waiting for you. The flowers are sending out their different perfumes and they blend into a lovely fragrance which the gentle wind takes into the air.

In the clearing is a very elegant piano, waiting

for you to seat yourself and play on the smooth black and white keys. Perhaps it is an upright piano with carved legs. Or perhaps it is a grand piano, not as high but sweeping back a long way with its top held up by a prop.

This piano would love to be played. It gets a little sad when no one takes any notice. The strings tighten and become set because they need fingers on the keys to make them work properly.

The seat in front matches the color of the piano. If you raise the lid, you will find books of music inside. Select the piece you would like to play and then sit on the seat with the music in front of you. Place your hands on the keys, look at the sheet of music, and play.

Your fingers move across the keyboard to the

rhythm of the music. Perhaps you thought you couldn't play, but listen. Music is pouring forth from the piano and your fingers. It is as though the two of you are one.

Instead of reading the music, why don't you, in your head, compose your own? Place your hands on the keys and think of what you would like to play. It is easy to take the thoughts from your head down into your fingers and then onto the keyboard.

And now you are playing your own music. Don't go too fast at first. Play some quiet medleys. Feel the music going out to people who like to listen to these magical tunes. Change the tempo. Make it fast and lively so that people want to dance. Change it yet again so that the music becomes strong and

deep, with your fingers racing up and down
the keys.

You feel happy playing the piano and want to
continue playing . . .

Perfection

THE AIR is fresh and clean, and the perfume of the flowers surrounds you as they bend their heads in the gentle breeze that has entered your garden.

There is a gate before you which I would like you to open. It is not a heavy gate but one which will open freely and easily as you push it lightly. It will open to the place which is where you want to be at this time.

Whatever you want to achieve is there for you if you see yourself as being perfect and becoming more perfect each and every day.

You might want to see yourself on a football field with thousands of people cheering you, even if you are not a footballer. Perhaps it is a hockey stadium where you rush to and fro with the puck or it could be tennis courts with people watching you score points again and again. Perhaps it is a polo match . . .

It could be a concert hall where you are performing the music or the dance that is special to you, or perhaps it is a rock concert where you have people in the palm of your hand, cheering you on.

It doesn't matter what it is or where it is, as

long as you see yourself fulfilling your dream. You may see yourself at a university or college accepting a diploma which you have worked hard to attain. Whatever you choose to do seems possible.

See yourself standing before these people. They rise to their feet and applaud. A feeling of love wells up inside you for them and for yourself, knowing that what you are doing is the right thing at this moment of time.

See yourself as being perfect. There are no faults, there are no problems, there are no limitations. All is well in your world . . .

Achievement

Sometimes achieving can be so difficult that we put the effort aside thinking "for another time" or "for tomorrow", but there is no need to wait. If you start to work now, in your meditations, on what you need to achieve you are putting things into a positive focus. Job interviews and passing exams are very stressful. See yourself being interviewed successfully, or passing those exams. We need to have a positive self-image and we can work on that in the meditative state.

Both **School** and **Exams** are examples of what we could do and what we could accomplish.

Floating allows your mind to expand and to encompass ideas you thought impossible.

School

YOUR GARDEN is peaceful and serene, the
sky a gentle blue with puffs of clouds drifting past.
There are many strawberry and mulberry bushes
with ripened fruit waiting to be picked. Perhaps you
could put some into a container and take them with
you as you wander down your pathway.

There is a building in front of you which is
framed by flowers and has gentle green ivy growing

up the walls and around the doorway. This is a place of learning which you will want to enter. If you walk down the corridors and look into each room, you will find the one that is right for you.

A teacher is at the blackboard explaining mathematics or how to punctuate a sentence. Perhaps it is even a laboratory where you are being taught scientific experiments and you put on a white coat and mix various formulas together.

Whatever it is that is being taught, see yourself as an absorbent sponge, able to take in all that is being said. More importantly, not only being able to take it in, but understanding exactly what is being said.

Keep listening to your teacher, watching the

movements and expressions as the finer points of the study in question are explained.

Your mind is analyzing, taking in and examining what it needs for the subject at hand, and discarding for another time that which is unnecessary.

Pick up the pencil and write how you feel and what you feel. Do you feel good about learning? Do you like your teacher? Do you want to learn more than you already know? And do you want to understand how the knowledge you are learning will be used when you leave school? Whatever questions you have regarding school or teachers or learning, write them down. How do you think your learning process could be improved?

Think about the things you would like to do

when you leave school. Do you want to go to university? Perhaps a technical college? Or a secretarial college? Know that whatever you want is within your grasp. You have the ability to take in what your teacher is saying, to absorb, to modify, to use, to bring out the best there is in you.

Pick up your pen and take a fresh sheet of paper. Start pulling up from your mind all the mathematical equations you can think of, the ones you thought so difficult and which you now find are pouring through so easily. Look at the English or French language with which you were having difficulty. Now you find it easy.

All because you allowed yourself to absorb the

knowledge imparted, to take it in and work with it on the inner level. Know that you can do anything you set your mind to do. Your mind shall not let you down . . .

Exams

THE PEACE and tranquility within your garden lies around you like a cloak, quietening and preparing you. The animals have come and perhaps you could stay with them for a time, feeling their peace and contentment, before you enter your place of learning.

It is nearly time to start the exam. You have enough time to settle down and relax before the clock will tell you to start.

Breathe in and feel the air going straight into your lungs, deeper and deeper. Let the air escape slowly, and then bring more air in. Take it from the top of the lungs to the bottom, and then reverse the air back out, feeling it flowing gently all the while.

Relax your body. See it sinking into a cushion of air and being supported by the air. Your adrenalin system is calm, your heartbeat strong and regular, and your breathing is slow. Your system is getting ready for the time when the hands of the clock move together.

Watch the clock's hands moving slowly around and know that when the hands are on the hour to start, you will be relaxed and ready to sit for your exam.

Look into your mind and know that you have

been working with your mind for a long time, working for this day. Your mind has been taking in, absorbing knowledge which is there for you to grasp, to bring forth, to answer the questions on the paper.

Look at your brain. Put it in front of you and you will see it pulsating with knowledge. Since you were born you have been storing all sorts of knowledge in this marvellous brain of yours. Know that it is marvellous, know that it is there for you to work with, and know that the knowledge it contains is yours.

One minute to go until you start writing. Check yourself over. Your breathing is fine, your body relaxed, and your mind is sharp, just waiting to be used.

And the time is now when you will bring forth all the wonderful things you have been taught, secure in the knowledge that you can do whatever you have set your mind to do, that you can accomplish all the goals you have set for yourself.

The paper is white and clean, your pencils freshly sharpened, your pens neatly lined up, and as the hands on the clock come together, you will take a pencil or pen in your hand, and write and write and write, never having to stop unless to turn the page over.

Your brain is running ahead of you and your hand flies over the page, answering question after question. The information is flying from your mind, to your hand, to the paper.

Know that when you have completed your test, there is only one thing to be said, and that is "Well done" . . .

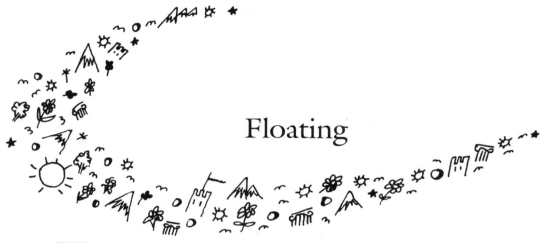

Floating

YOUR GARDEN is full of mystical beauty and has a quality which is dreamlike. There is nothing you cannot do. Whatever you wish to do is there for you, but first you must unshackle your thinking and allow your thoughts to expand so they encompass ideas which you thought impossible.

The grass beneath your feet is lovely and soft, yet rich in its texture and color. Look at the ground and at your feet and you will notice that slowly, very slowly, your feet are coming off the ground. There is distance between the soles of your feet and the earth. The distance is increasing so that you are now hovering over the grass. Now you can go deeper into your garden without touching a blade of grass.

Feel yourself gliding forward until you come to the seashore. Because your feet are not touching the ground, you cannot feel the sand beneath them. Go forward until you reach the water and watch the waves coming in and out as you rise above them. As the waves get higher, you can raise yourself up further. When they flatten themselves out, you can come down so that you are just above them. Keep doing this and you will ride the waves in and out without getting your feet wet. When you get tired of this, come back across the beach and return to your garden.

Go to a part of your garden which is special to you. Hover for a while as you look around and then, gently, see your feet settling back onto the ground. Wriggle your toes into the earth and feel its warmth on the soles of your feet.

Find a grassy spot which is spongy and lie down, feeling your body settling into the grass. The grass is a cushion which supports your body, surrounding it, so that you can sink into it more deeply than before. Relax and enjoy the comfort and the smell of the rich grass . . .

Overcoming Obstacles

Obstacles always occur at some point in life for all of us. No one is immune. We learn and we grow from these obstacles. One of the main lessons is to look at our difficulties and to learn how to overcome them. Why are they there? How should I look at them? What can I do?

The Mountain gives you a way of looking at these problems from different vantage points.

Father Time takes us back into our past, and also forward into our future. Can we change our future? Perhaps if we learn to resolve problems in an easier fashion, the future will not be as difficult.

The Mountain

THE GRASS is cool beneath your feet and the trees are tall and in full leaf. The breeze gently ruffles their branches and moves lightly through your hair as you walk down your pathway.

As you go further forward, you will see a mountain that is the biggest you have ever seen. It has many trees and rocks and the colorful wild flowers thrust themselves forward through the crevices. Why don't you climb this mountain to see what it feels like to climb the biggest mountain in the world?

You could walk up the small pathway which winds through the trees or you could climb the sheer rock face on the far side. Perhaps you may care to take the ski lift which many people use to get to the top?

Why don't you walk up the pathway? That way you will see the small mountain animals that live there. You would miss them if you climbed the rock face or took the ski lift.

You will find it becomes easier and easier to climb as you go up. It is not as steep as you thought. You can hear the rustling of small animals in the brush as they peek out to see who is treading the path. Some of them will show themselves to you. Others will hide because they are so very shy.

You are now at the top of the mountain and able to look down. Can you see where you started your journey? It's a long way down, isn't it? Look in front of you and you will see the earth laid out around you with many villages and farms. You can see people from here but they look very small, more like little dots moving around.

When you feel it is time to return to the bottom of the mountain, you could get into a mountain sled and race down the track until you reach your starting point.

And now I want you to see yourself becoming

bigger and bigger. You are growing at an enormous rate and, as you grow, you find the mountain, which you thought was so large, is now like a tiny hill. Throw your head back and laugh, and your laughter will be like rolling thunder across the earth.

Feel your long legs taking huge strides. Because you are now so tall, you have the perfect vantage point to see all that goes on. Because you are so tall, you will find that you can look at the mountain and wonder why you found it difficult to climb. You can use your mind in the same way. By expanding it, you can see your problems in a different light and from a different aspect.

Perhaps you might like to shrink until you are back to your normal size so that you can look at the mountain yet again in a different light. It wasn't that hard to climb in the first place, was it? And yet, when you changed size you had a different perspective of what was there.

I shall leave you with your mountain. You might want to stay small, or you might want to experiment with your size. It is up to you . . .

Father Time

THERE **IS** a feeling of serenity as you enter your garden, a serenity that makes you feel as though time is ageless, as though it is standing still.

If you would like to investigate time, why don't you go toward the large building in front of you which is made out of sandstone blocks. These blocks are very big and there are carvings on them which depict events that have happened, and events that will happen.

There are many steps to take you up towards tall, round pillars. When you walk between them, you will see a large doorway in front of you. The door is open.

Framed in the doorway is a man in white, flowing robes caught at the shoulder by a large clasp. On his feet are brown leather sandals to match the belt tied loosely around his waist. His thick hair is white and long and falls around his shoulders. His bushy beard is also white with a bit of ginger streaking through. His eyes are a brilliant sky blue and his face has lines which deepen as he smiles at you. When he smiles everything in his face lights up with pleasure and with love.

He is holding out his hand towards you. Why don't you approach him and take his hand, for he is

Father Time. He loves all people equally and he always has time to spare for those who visit him.

He is taking you inside the building, explaining how this building has stood the test of time, and is filled with many wonderful things for you to look at. Some of the rooms show the history of the earth from the very beginning of time. Some show ancient civilizations which no longer exist. And some show the earth as we know it today.

There are rooms which hold books and more books, too many to read in one lifetime. Because you are in your meditative or dream state, you can read as many of these books as you like.

Father Time is happy to answer any or all of your questions because he has all the time in the world to spend with you. There is no rush, no hurry. This gentle man has many children and adults visit so that he can explain how the earth was formed and where our civilization is today.

He is now taking you into a special part of this unusual building. Here he will show you the future. It is the future you can have if you choose, the future which is there if you work towards it.

I think I will leave you with him so that you can learn to understand the essence of time . . .

Healing and Perspective

These meditations can be used to change the way you feel about yourself, your past life, or other people. Going into a meditative state and healing yourself is a wonderful way of dealing with hurts or feelings of inadequacy or loss. I believe that we can heal many things through meditation and there are instances of people healing themselves through constant application of positive thought combined with meditation. You may find that these meditations will dissolve and dissipate tension and bring a calmness and serenity to you which you may not have experienced for some time.

The Heart shows you the many rooms that exist within, the rooms of happiness and the rooms where you have stored various hurts and sorrows.

The Reflecting Pool asks that you look at yourself and see yourself as you are inside.

The Tortoise shows that perhaps your sensitivity is hidden away and maybe you should look at it.

Your Day of Birth takes you back to when you were a speck in the universe. This meditation then brings you forward into this world with your special day of birth.

The Boulevard of Broken Dreams takes you back into the past where you must heal the past in order to go on into the future.

The Colors of Healing takes you through a wonderful mirage of colors which are healing for the body and the mind.

The Heart

THERE ARE many daffodils and primroses in your garden, and their perfume drifts into the cloudless sky. It settles around the many colored birds that sit on the branches of the Grandfather Tree, the oldest tree in your garden. There is a small seat with a padded cushion near the thick trunk. Why don't you sit on this seat and examine your heart?

If you put your heart in front of you, you can

observe its beauty as you watch it growing larger and larger. Its color is bright red and it is pulsating at an even rate. As you watch, you will see a small door which will take you inside. I want you to see yourself growing smaller and smaller so that you can pass through this door and enter your heart. You will notice that the door has a keyhole but you have no need of a key for you do not lock your heart away.

For those people who do, the keyhole may have become rusted and might need a tear or two to melt the rust and allow the key to open the lock. Tears can release so many things within us, and sometimes it is necessary to allow them to flow.

Your heart keeps pumping in a regular manner as you open the door. Entering your heart will feel strange at first. Now that you are inside can you feel the beat? You are moving up and down, up and down with your beats. You will become used to the movement in a little while.

There are rooms within your heart which you might care to enter. One room is filled with happiness, another with joy, and yet another with love.

There are also rooms which show how the heart can be hurt or wounded by uncaring or unkind words. It is good to go into these rooms to understand the hurt that is there and then return into the rooms of happiness, love and joy. The more time you spend in these rooms, the more able you will be to not only receive love, but to give it wholeheartedly, understanding that the other rooms exist.

Some people are not aware that they can enter their heart in this way. Because you are aware, you might be able to share with them your ability to enter at ease.

The more time you spend in these rooms, the more you will understand the heart's flow and capacity for love. The more love you give the more you are able to receive . . .

The Reflecting Pool

GO FORWARD along the path before you.
Feel as always the peace and quiet and serenity
which exist there. Smell the freshness of the flowers.
Perhaps you could pluck one, placing it into your
lapel or behind your ear. You will see another flower
forming to take the place of the one you have taken
because in your garden nothing dies.

The path has taken you to a round clearing.

In the centre is a pool which has rough brick surrounding the edges, and a stone flattened to form a seat. Look how clear the water is, how smooth, with just a faint breeze stirring the waters. Why don't you sit with your feet dangling into the pool. See how the water changes when you stir it with your feet?

If you sit quietly, the water will become calm and reflect your image back to you like a glass mirror. I wonder what you see? You can see your physical appearance of course, the shape of your head, the slant of your shoulders, and the wisps of hair straying in the breeze.

If you become very quiet and still, and if you look deeper and deeper into the pool, you will see a depth to the waters that you have not noticed before. Feel yourself going deeper and deeper. Do not enter the waters yet, just feel the images reflecting the changing essence of who you are. Perhaps you see a person revealed as being able and complete for others, or perhaps you see the "you" whom no one else can see, the one that hides inside. Why don't you reflect into your pool what you want to be? Sometimes it can be difficult to see yourself as you really are because we can be colored by other people's perceptions.

Stay by the edge of the pool and feel the sun's warmth on your body. Notice that the sun is not only warming the outer body but also penetrating the inner being which needs light and warmth.

This pool will enable you to reach depths within yourself that you have never reached before.

You do not need to enter the waters unless you would like to. You can feel the changes starting within as you sit there, changes that are necessary if you are to feel more complete, more sure, more able. This pool will reflect back to you an image, not only of who you are now, but who and what you can be . . .

The Tortoise

IT **IS** very quiet and peaceful in your garden. Feel the freshness of the air and the serenity there. The animals are coming forward to greet you. Perhaps there is one from your past, a favorite dog, cat or bird; maybe even a parrot. Or you might choose to see an animal which would normally not come close to you. All the animals co-exist peacefully in your garden and they like being called forward when people enter their special place.

Now what do I see coming towards you very slowly? It's a tortoise! He has been sunning himself and his shell is very warm to touch. Why don't you place your hand there and feel that warmth? He is turning his head to watch you as you stroke the shell.

He is rather lonely at times and most people do not understand that tortoises pull their heads in because they become frightened. He is moving very slowly away from you, going along the garden path. The other animals are moving very quickly, their feet going in all directions as they hurry towards the watering hole.

Why don't you join the tortoise and walk with him towards the watering hole? It seems to me that you could learn a lot from him. He protects his sensitivity by hiding under his shell, yet perhaps that shell should be removed to show what is underneath. He appears to be slow and ponderous—but he always gets there in the end. As he walks he absorbs what is happening around him. He notices how he feels within himself, how he feels towards his environment.

Perhaps you could put on a shell and very slowly make your way alongside him. You might find it is no longer necessary to hurry, nor to hide how you feel. Take your time with this magnificent creature, and you will reach your destination at the time that is right for you . . .

Your Day of Birth

FEEL THE freshness of the grass and the dew beneath your feet as you go forward into your garden. Breathe in the aroma from the flowers drifting towards you on the light breeze. Let the powdery clouds against the velvet blue of the sky bring to mind your Day of Birth. Imagine that you chose that particular moment in time to be born.

Birthdays are very special days because they

celebrate our Day of Birth. It is as if the planets were frozen for that moment as we made our entrance. Our Day of Birth makes us unique and different from each other, and yet we are alike in what we do. We walk, we talk, we think, we act, we sleep, we eat, and we feel—but it is in the feeling that we become different from each other.

Imagine that before you were born you were a little speck in the universe until you looked down and decided which family to be born into. I believe we have free will to make these decisions and to choose the parents to whom we think we should belong. If that is so, perhaps you saw your mother and father from above and watched them until it was time for you to descend to be a living and breathing entity who grew over the nine month period until it was time for your birth.

It was so comfortable in your mother's womb that sometimes you wished you did not have to emerge because she carried you everywhere. You could hear the conversations she had with your father and how they longed for your presence in their world so that they could love you and cuddle you and make you their very own.

And so you decided to make their world yours, and you arrived. Some things you didn't like and you cried in a baby's way, "give me lots of cuddles because I have come such a long way to be with you".

Your new parents looked at you with deep expressions of love and also with surprise that they could have brought such a tiny bundle of joy into this world, one who would stay with them and bring them happiness as you grew. This happiness was tinged with the sadness of the knowledge that you would eventually leave them to make your own way in life. But the love you have for each other can live on. There is no need for such love to die or to change simply because you have gone your own way.

For some, recalling their Day of Birth is a sad experience, perhaps because they had no one to love them as completely as they needed, or because they were abandoned or excluded in some way. To heal and enjoy your own special day, you may need to let go by seeing your mother or father as tiny specks in the universe who, like you looked down from above and decided who their birth parents were to be . . .

The Boulevard of Broken Dreams

IT IS quiet when you enter your garden and you can feel the peace and the solitude surrounding you, supporting you as you look back on your past life, on the happy times, and perhaps the times that were not so happy.

Life has brought you experiences of intense joy and happiness. Perhaps it has also given you periods of equally intense sadness. Sometimes it is necessary to go back into the past to discover what it is that makes life difficult at this point in time.

Why don't you go far back into your own past, to the time when you were a small child, and see yourself with your family. When your parents had to leave you to attend a function, were you a little sad? Or did you cope with it well? Remember the times you had arguments at school and people upset you to the point when you could not eat and you cried and cried. Remember also the times when you laughed and enjoyed the companionship of your childhood friends around you.

Why don't you come further forward now from this period to a time as a teenager when you were very vulnerable. Perhaps you could look at the insecurities you felt. How the world seemed such a large place in comparison to the security of your home. Perhaps you also experienced anger as a teenager when you were neither child nor adult and you found it difficult to enjoy the earlier childish pleasures yet you were not old enough to fully embrace adult life.

As an adult, you may have come into a time when perhaps the dreams you had as a child should have come to fruition but, for some reason, didn't. This may be because of circumstances or perhaps because you did not extend yourself in the way you should have. Perhaps you feel sad because you didn't take advantage of what was there for you.

Your sensitive inner core may have been hurt because your love was rejected but perhaps you could look at this and release the hurt that you have held close.

I want you to go back to each experience, to look at it carefully, and to be impartial. Instead of looking at how some particular person or circumstance has hurt you, look instead at what you have learned. Don't allocate or accept blame. Don't worry about what this person said or did or what you said or did. Look only at what you feel yourself and how you can bring into your present life a positive result from what you have experienced before.

Instead of the anger, the blame, the denial, the guilt, look at the love, the acceptance, and the tolerance which you have learned to give to the people around you.

Don't deny the experiences you have had, but also don't keep them closely around you. Each experience is a learning experience which teaches us to let go, to release.

Go within your heart for your experiences and look at them closely. Take from them the positive aspects that you need to work with and release those that are no longer of use.

Can you learn to release, to be non-judgmental, and to love without requiring love in return? Try to do this and you will find yourself giving, and in the giving, you will receive . . .

The Colors of Healing

THE BLUE of the sky is enriched by the svelte green of the trees thrusting their branches and leaves high into the air. The birds dart to and fro, picking up little twigs to build nests to settle into, within the comfort and security of the trees' branches.

The air is so fresh in your garden that your lungs have no difficulty in expanding and contracting as they take in this precious commodity.

Draw the air deep into the very bottom of your lungs, and then send it back out again, forcing out the old air which has stayed for so long without being expelled.

You feel much better for breathing deeply. In, out, in, out, always taking the fresh air through the lungs and ridding yourself of the stale and the old.

The oxygen is giving you a sense of well being, a sense of wanting to leap forward, to jump for joy. But are you really ready for it? I think you have to work more on your body before you can take off in the way you would like.

Lie down on the spongy green grass and feel the way the grass cushions your body holding you just above the earth. Keep breathing deeply and feel the impact of the air cleansing your lungs.

Because your lungs are feeling so healthy with this lovely clean air coursing through them, you could start to heal your body by thinking of various colors.

Feel comfortable and secure resting above your grassy bed while you surround yourself with the healing color of blue. See this blue as a mist forming around you and penetrating the pores of you skin, entering the body. This blue is going to touch every organ within your body until each organ is filled with this blue and cleansed. Take your time and feel the color as it touches you and heals the organs that need healing. There is no need to hurry. You have all the time in the world to take these colors through your body. Breathe this blue through your body, and feel it expanding throughout your system, cleansing and healing.

Bring through next the healing color of green. See the green as a mist forming around your body and penetrating the pores, taking it through your body so that it heals and regenerates those areas that are in need. Always take your time. There is no need to hurry for it is necessary for these colors to be absorbed into your system. Breathe this green through your body, cleansing and healing your system, making you feel alert and vital.

Look at your blood stream and see how sluggish it is. Bring through a brilliant red, and take it coursing through your system, brightening and energizing those areas which are in need. See this red cleansing the network of veins and arteries and purifying them, making them whole and complete.

Go into you heart and see how it pulsates.

Take the color red through each section and notice how it cleanses, purifies and ensures that the pumping action is once again pure and clean and strong. Feel the strength of your heart as it throbs, taking this red into each and every vital part of your body.

And now, take through a gentle pink to enable your heart to love freely and completely. Feel that beautiful pink permeating the whole of your heart. See your heart opening like a gentle pink flower, full and complete, with love to spare not only for others, but also for yourself.

For the mind, use the color yellow. Take it through each segment of the brain and see each part glow as it receives and uses this golden color, cleansing the negative thoughts, and removing them from your consciousness. Take your time with this lovely golden light as you purify and cleanse your mind. Feel the clarity within your mind as the negativity is removed and the golden light moves through, highlighting the areas that were in need.

Surround your body with cleansing white light and know you have purified your body, that the healing has commenced. Bring this pure white light in a steady stream through your body, feeling it in every part. Wash it around you and pour it through your system so that you feel cleansed and whole.

And now bring through the color purple, the highest of the spiritual colors. Bring it through and around you as a light mist which is deepening until the color purple is strong and alive and glows.

Surround yourself with this beautiful purple, see it entering every section of your being and feel the upliftment and peace it brings and know that your body and mind are well and at peace . . .

Also by Maureen Garth

Maureen Garth's first collection of meditations for children, *Starbright*, attracted an immediate world-wide response from parents, teachers and the children themselves.

This second collection of children's stories, *Moonbeam*, will further help children to learn meditation from an early age. They will find their concentration improved, their creative abilities enhanced, and their capacity to deal with anxieties strengthened.

Maureen Garth shows parents how to use these imaginings with their children and to discover unsuspected benefits both for the children and for themselves.

"Nurturing in children a sense that they are never alone, that they are in loving company always, and can always find that caring presence in their hearts, may be the most subtle but precious gift we can bestow on them. These simple exercises, with their straightforward, gentle language, helped this concerned parent begin to do just that."

Phil Catalfo, *New Dimensions*

HarperCollins*Publishers*

ISBN 1 86371 142 2

Also by Maureen Garth

Maureen first devised creative visualisations to help her three year old daughter feel secure and cared for. *Starbright* is a collection of innovative meditations that parents and carers can read to their children to help them sleep, develop concentration, awaken creativity, and learn to quiet themselves.

Innerspace is a collection of creative visualisations written to help teenagers meet the challenges of growing, learning and living. There are 25 original meditations which deal with overcoming peer group pressure, passing exams and setting goals.

 HarperCollins*Publishers*